Fast and Easy
C++ Lessons

In This Edition:
Preprocessing
On Microsoft
Visual Studio Code
in Linux Ubuntu

Zlatin Georgiev

Version 1.1, 2024-02-17

Table Of Contents

Copyright

Dedication

This book is for those who like to learn new and interesting things.

Introduction

This book will teach you practically:

- How to install tools to build 32-bit and 64-bit **C** and **C++** applications, which is important to correctly reproduce all the examples in the book;

- What are **C** and **C++** compiler preprocessor directives;

- How you can use them to write code that compiles applications for different operating systems or different processor architectures;

- A brief understanding of commands from the bash scripting language used to automate operations by the operating system;

and many more.

In addition, in separate chapters, the book contains detailed explanations of the sample **C++** program code and the batch scripts used.

All examples in this book were tested on a computer with the **Ubuntu version 22.04.3** operating system at the time immediately before publication.

The installation of the necessary tools for compiling and editing **C** and **C++** programs has been carefully tested (✓), in case there is a problem with the installation, please double-check the installation script texts and confirm you have typed them in correctly. Make sure you have carefully followed the instructions in the book.

The examples are tested (✓) for fluent compilation. In case they do not compile or run, it would be good to make sure the input you have entered matches with that in the book.

The output results correspond to the examples used (there may be differences in rare cases when some non-standard symbols or graphic characters are output).

The following bookmarks are used in the book:

i   to note

♀   a piece of advice

🔥   bring to attention

⚠️   warning

❗   of importance

Chapter 1. Installing tools for compiling and editing C++ programs

1.1. Installing Linux C++ building tools

To install the necessary tools, press the key combination Ctrl + Alt + T, through which we open the **Linux Terminal**, in which we enter:

> If the **Linux Terminal** does not open:
> **1**. Press the key combination Ctrl + Alt + F3.
> **2**. Log in as root with your root password.
> **3**. Enter the nano /etc/default/locale and inside the text editor change everywhere the en_US to the en_US.UTF-8 and press Ctrl + S to save your changes.
> **4**. After that press Ctrl + X to exit the text editor.
> **5**. Execute the locale-gen --purge command and reboot to restart the **Linux Ubuntu** operating system.

Listing 1. Linux Terminal

```
echo ${USER}
```

The result of this command is the current <user name>. We will use this user name to add the user to the sudoers group with administrator privileges.

Listing 2. Linux Terminal

```
su -
usermod -aG sudo "<the user name from the above echo command>"
reboot
```

After rebooting in a **Linux Terminal**, we enter the command:

Listing 3. Linux Terminal

```
sudo apt -y update
```

After the execution of the above command, we enter the password with which we log in as a user in **Ubuntu** in response to the message [sudo] password for developer: and press the Enter key.

Listing 4. Linux Terminal

```
sudo apt -y install build-essential
```

The above command installs:

- g++ the GNU compiler for **C++** programs;
- gcc the GNU compiler for **C** programs;
- make utility that is used for directing the building of programs;

  and possibly the gdb debugger for Linux

programs.

Listing 5. Linux Terminal

```
sudo apt -y install gdb
```

The above command installs the gdb GNU debugger.

See the appendixes to find out how you can install a newer version of **GCC** than the one installed by default for your particular version of **Linux**:

- Appendix A, *Installing a newer release version of the GNU Compiler Collection (GCC)*
- Appendix B, *Installing the latest version of the GNU Compiler Collection (GCC)*

1.1.1. Checking the C++ compiler is properly working

We check if the compiler, for **C++** programs, is properly installed:

We check the **C++** compiler version:

Listing 6. Linux Terminal

```
g++ --version
```

The result we get should look something like this:

Example 1. Default g++ version for **Linux Ubuntu** 22.04 LTS

```
g++ (Ubuntu 11.3.0-1ubuntu1~22.04) 11.3.0
Copyright (C) 2021 Free Software Foundation, Inc.
This is free software; see the source for copying conditions.  There is NO
warranty; not even for MERCHANTABILITY or FITNESS FOR A PARTICULAR PURPOSE.
```

 For the **Linux Ubuntu** 18.x the result looks like the next one:

Example 2. Default g++ version for **Linux Ubuntu** 18.04 LTS

```
g++ (Ubuntu 7.5.0-3ubuntu1~18.04) 7.5.0
Copyright (C) 2017 Free Software Foundation, Inc.
This is free software; see the source for copying conditions.  There is NO
warranty; not even for MERCHANTABILITY or FITNESS FOR A PARTICULAR PURPOSE.
```

Then in the command window, we write:

Listing 7. Linux Terminal

```
which g++
```

to check if the compiler, for **C++** programs, is installed.

Example 3. The result should look something like this:

```
/usr/bin/g++
```

1.1.2. Creating and compiling a C++ Hello World application

The next thing we'll do is create a folder in which to place the `hello_world` application source code with the command:

Listing 8. Linux Terminal

```
mkdir -p ~/c++/sources/chapter_01_01_02/step_01
```

Then we enter the newly created folder:

Listing 9. Linux Terminal

```
cd ~/c++/sources/chapter_01_01_02/step_01
```

In this folder, we create the `hello_world.cpp` file:

Listing 10. Linux Terminal

```
nano hello_world.cpp
```

Listing 11.
`~/c++/sources/chapter_01/step_01_01_02/hello_world.cpp`

```cpp
#include <iostream>

using namespace std;

int main() {
  cout << "Hello World!\n";
}
```

We enter the code of the program and save it with the keys `Ctrl` + `S`, then we exit the text editor with `Ctrl` + `X`.

We compile the test program with the command:

Listing 12. Linux Terminal

```
g++ -o hello_world hello_world.cpp
```

then we launch it

Listing 13. Linux Terminal

```
./hello_world
```

Example 4. The result displayed on the screen should be:

```
Hello World!
```

In this way, we verified that we have an environment in which we can create programs written in the programming language **C++**.

After successfully installing the necessary tools to write and compile **C** and **C++** programs for the **Linux** operating system we can proceed to install **Microsoft Visual Studio Code** - a tool for editing and debugging **C++** source code.

Now I will briefly explain what each line of the above program means:

```
#include <iostream>
```

This line loads the **C++** function descriptions to work with input/output streams - in this case, the function `cout`

```
using namespace std;
```

This line specifies that we can use functions from the `std` namespace without specifying their full name, in this case, we can use `cout` instead of `std::cout`, which makes the program code more readable.

 Defaulting to the `std` namespace is bad practice, as this is the **Standard Template Library** namespace of **C++**. The above way of setting default namespaces can be used for namespaces belonging to the particular application being developed.

```
int main() {
```

This line indicates the beginning of the entry point function in the **C++** program. This is the function named `main` which returns an integer `int`. It does not accept input parameters in its current declaration.

> The `main` function can also be declared with two input parameters, one of which specifies the number of arguments passed from the command line of the program, and the other the parameters themselves in the form of an array of strings - for example, `int main(int arguments_count, char* arguments [])` or `int main(int arguments_count, char** arguments)`.

```
cout << "Hello World!\n";
```

This line from the body of the `main` function outputs the `Hello World!` message that we see in the command window after the program is executed.

```
}
```

This line ends the body of the `main` function.

1.2. Installing the Microsoft Visual Studio Code

We will install **Microsoft Visual Studio Code** using the **snap** tool.

1.2.1. Installing the Microsoft Visual Studio Code using the Snap tool

1. We open a new **Linux Terminal** with the key combination `Ctrl` + `Alt` + `T`:

2. Before we start the actual installation of **Microsoft Visual Studio Code** we will prepare two settings files that we will need to compile **C++** programs.

   a. We create the folder `~/c++/.vscode`:

   Listing 14. Linux Terminal

   ```
   mkdir -p ~/c++/.vscode
   ```

   b. and the file `~/c++/.vscode/tasks.json`

   Listing 15. Linux Terminal

   ```
   nano ~/c++/.vscode/tasks.json
   ```

    When using 64-bit operating system **Linux Ubuntu** version 18.04.6 in the script below you should replace c++20 with c++17 everywhere. Because in this case the default build-essential installs the g++ version 7.5.0 and it supports the c++17 standard and below.

with the following content:

Listing 16. `~/c++/.vscode/tasks.json`

```json
{
  "tasks": [
    {
      "type": "cppbuild",
      "label": "C/C++: g++ build active file",
      "command": "/usr/bin/g++",
      "args": [
        "-std=c++20",
        "-Wfatal-errors",
        "-fdiagnostics-color=always",
        "-lstdc++",
        "-I.",
        "-g",
        "${file}",
        "-o",
        "${fileDirname}/${fileBasenameNoExtension}"
      ],
      "options": {
        "cwd": "${fileDirname}"
      },
      "problemMatcher": [
        "$gcc"
      ],
      "group": {
        "kind": "build",
        "isDefault": true
      },
      "detail": "Task generated by Debugger."
    }
  ],
  "version": "2.0.0"
}
```

and save it with Ctrl + S and you can close the nano text editor with Ctrl + X .

c. We also create the file `~/c++/.vscode/launch.json` in the same folder:

Listing 17. Linux Terminal

```
nano ~/c++/.vscode/launch.json
```

and in it, we enter the following content:

Listing 18. `~/c++/.vscode/launch.json`

```
{
  "version": "0.2.0",
  "configurations": [
    {
      "name": "(gdb) Launch",
      "type": "cppdbg",
      "request": "launch",
      "program": "${fileDirname}/${fileBasenameNoExtension}",
      "args": [],
      "stopAtEntry": false,
      "cwd": "${workspaceFolder}",
      "externalConsole": false,
      "MIMode": "gdb",
      "setupCommands": [
        {
          "description": "Enable pretty-printing for gdb",
          "text": "-enable-pretty-printing",
          "ignoreFailures": true
        },
        {
          "description": "Set Disassembly Flavor to Intel",
          "text": "-gdb-set disassembly-flavor intel",
          "ignoreFailures": true
        }
      ],
      "additionalSOLibSearchPath": "",
      "preLaunchTask": "C/C++: g++ build active file"
    }
  ]
}
```

and save it with `Ctrl` + `S`. After that close the `nano` text editor with `Ctrl` + `X`.

d. Then we create a configuration file for automatic formatting of C++ source code `~/c++/.clang-format`

Listing 19. Administrator: Linux Terminal

```
nano ~/c++/.clang-format
```

with content:

Listing 20. `~/c++/.clang-format`

```
---
Language:       Cpp
BasedOnStyle:   Chromium
ColumnLimit:    120
UseTab:         Never
---
Language:       Json
IndentWidth:    1
...
```

and save it using the key combination `Ctrl` + `S` and close the `nano` text editor with `Ctrl` + `X`.

3. Next, we install **Microsoft Visual Studio Code** using **snap**

Listing 21. Linux Terminal

```
sudo apt -y install snapd
sudo snap install --classic code
```

4. When the installation is finished we install the extension to **Microsoft Visual Studio Code**, which allows us to compile and debug

C++ programs.

Listing 22. Linux Terminal

```
code --install-extension ms-vscode.cpptools-extension-pack
```

ℹ️ Installing the extensions this way, from the command line, allows you to automate the process with the help of scripts for the operating system, so you will easily have all the extensions that are convenient and necessary for you to work, even if you have to reinstall **Microsoft Visual Studio Code**.

5. Then we run **Microsoft Visual Studio Code** so that it opens the folder ~/c++ and the file hello_world.cpp:

Listing 23. Linux Terminal

```
code ~/c++ ~/c++/sources/chapter_01_01_02/step_01/hello_world.cpp
```

ℹ️ This is a very convenient feature of **Microsoft Visual Studio Code** that allows you to launch it with the working folder and file you need to edit, directly from the command line, without having to specify them later in the working environment itself with a mouse or keyboard commands. For example, you can make a script that automates the opening of a working folder and file for each of the applications you develop.

6. At the first launch, we will answer to the question `Do you trust the authors of the files in the folder?` with pressing the `[Yes, I trust the authors]` button:

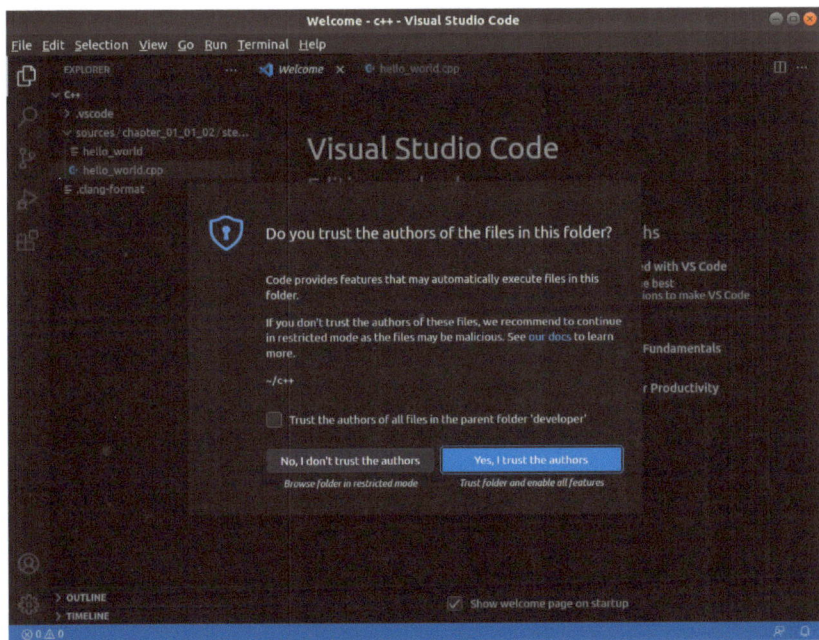

Figure 1. Do you trust the authors of the files in the folder?

7. After that the `Welcome` screen of the program appears and we close it with `Ctrl` + `W`:

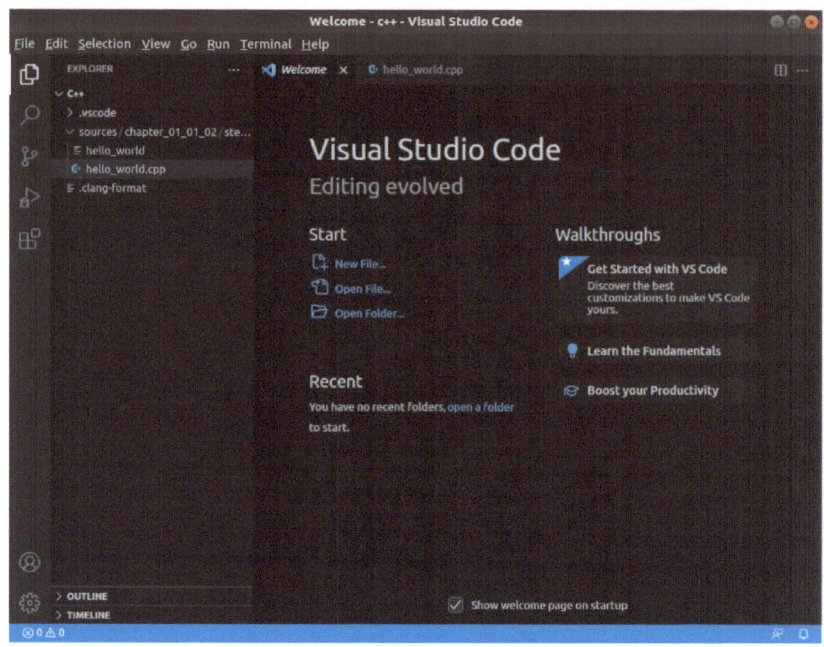

Figure 2. **Microsoft Visual Studio Code** *Welcome screen*

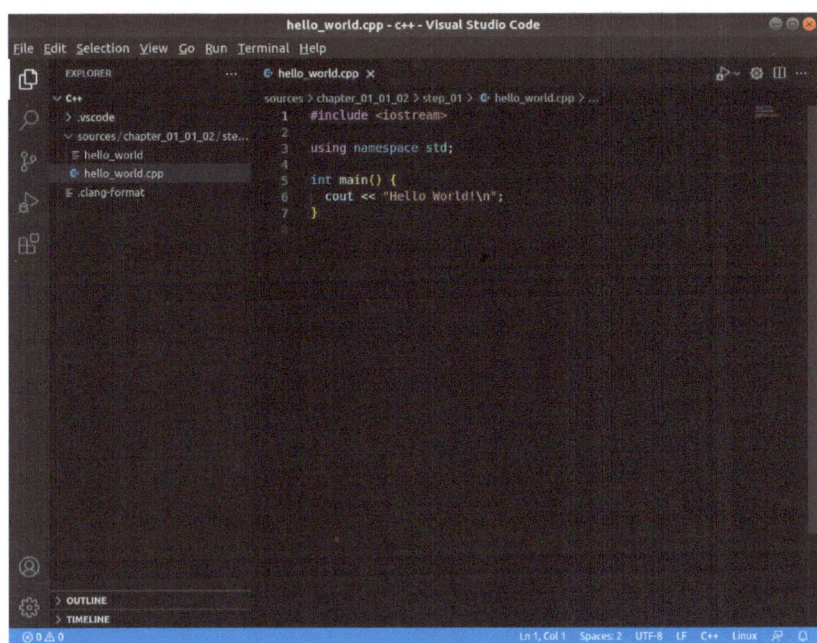

Figure 3. **Microsoft Visual Studio Code** *opening*
`hello_world.cpp`

8. Then we press the F5 key, which will allow us to compile the program and run it in trace mode. We will see execution in the `DEBUG CONSOLE`:

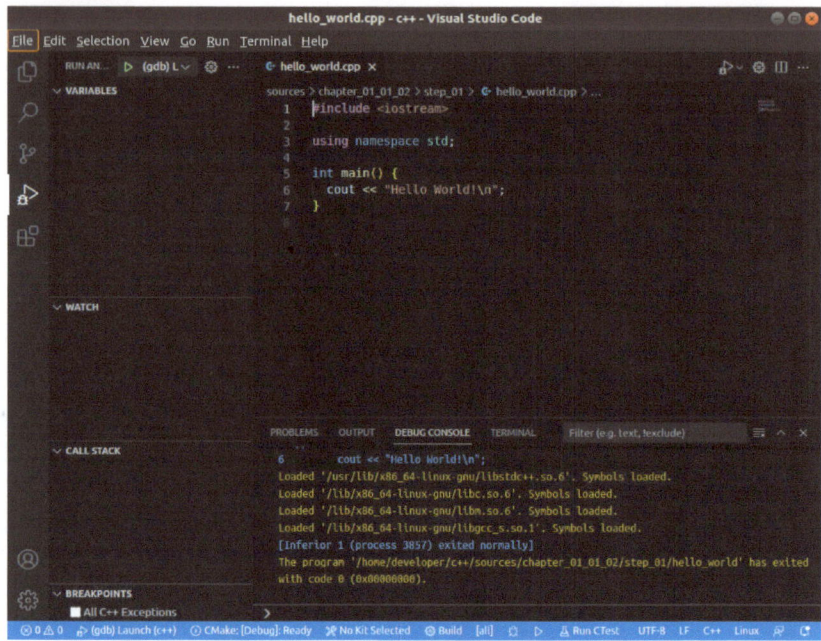

Figure 4. Run with the F5 key in the debug console

9. We will see the result of the execution of the Hello World! program in the Microsoft Visual Studio Code TERMINAL window by clicking the [left mouse button] on it.

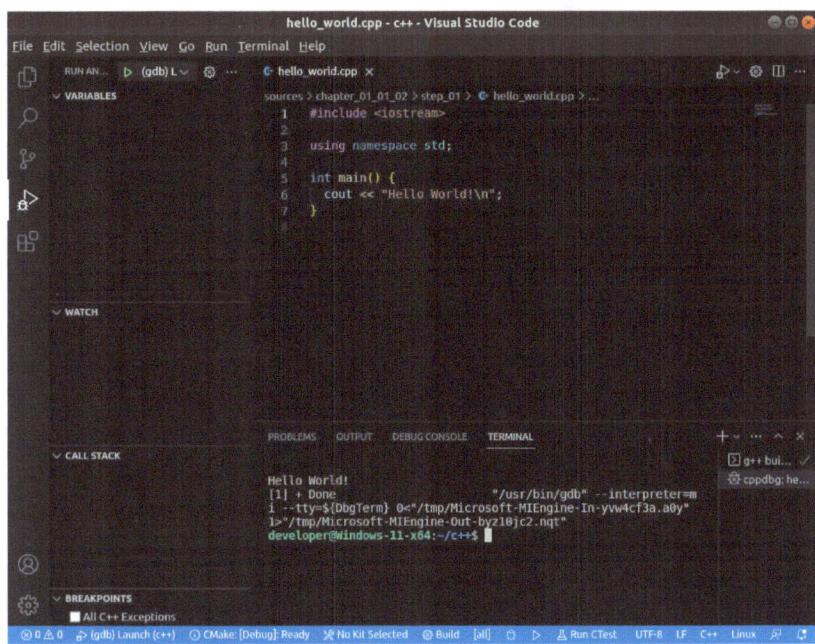

Figure 5. **Microsoft Visual Studio Code** *terminal window*

If we want to trace the execution of a program, we simply click the [left mouse button] in front of the number of the line at which we want the execution to stop and there appears a red dot - a breakpoint. Then we press the F5 key again and the program compiles to an executable again and stops its execution at the line with the red dot. To continue execution:

- We can press F5 again to continue to the next breakpoint or until the end of the program.

- We can also use the F10 key to execute the code of the current line and stop the execution of the next line.

- It is also possible to use the `F11` key to examine the execution of the current function.

If we want to remove a breakpoint, we simply click the `[ left mouse button ]` on the red dot and it disappears.

Having successfully installed the necessary tools for compiling and tracing **C++** programs will allow us to compile all the examples in this book.

Chapter 2. Preprocessing - preliminary processing

Preprocessing in **C++** is the application of a set of commands starting with the **#** character and making changes to the source program code before it is compiled by the compiler. Typically these are code injections, using one code instead of another based on different conditions and values of a special preprocessor variables.

The main preprocessor commands are as follows:

1. #define
2. #elif
3. #else
4. #endif
5. #error
6. #if
7. #ifdef

8. `#ifndef`

9. `#include`

10. `#line`

11. `#pragma`

12. `#undef`

13. `#warning`

In the following sections, we will look at each of the commands. We'll use, in addition to the traditional approach, one with **C++** explanations and examples to see how the preprocessor definitions and commands are converted to final source code that compiles from *C++ * the compiler to machine code so that it can be executed by the processor. In practice, when we start the compiler, it first executes the preprocessor commands that form the source code into the form from which the compiler compiles it and converts it to machine code. The process is as follows:

1. Source code + preprocessor commands.

2. Clean source code.

3. Machine code and possibly assembly code when an option is specified to the compiler to generate it.

2.1. #define

This directive defines a name that can then be used in the program's source code or by other preprocessor directives.

I will show you real examples of **C++** programs about how the #define preprocessor command does.

We create a folder in which to put the source code of the program.

Listing 24. Linux Terminal

```
mkdir -p ~/c++/sources/chapter_02_01_00/define_01
```

Then we enter the newly created folder.

Listing 25. Linux Terminal

```
cd ~/c++/sources/chapter_02_01_00/define_01
```

In this folder, we create the files preprocess.hpp and main.cpp

Listing 26. Linux Terminal

```
code preprocess.hpp main.cpp
```

With the following content:

Listing 27. chapter_02_01_00\define_01\preprocess.hpp

```cpp
#define DEFINED_MESSAGE "TEST"
#define EXIT_SUCCESS 0

const char* const MESSAGE = DEFINED_MESSAGE;
const int RESULT = EXIT_SUCCESS;
```

Listing 28. chapter_02_01_00\define_01\main.cpp

```cpp
#include <iostream>
#include "preprocess.hpp"

int main() {
  std::cout << MESSAGE << std::endl;

  return RESULT;
}
```

We perform preprocessing by sequentially executing the commands:

We enter the folder with the source code of the program.

Listing 29. Linux Terminal:

```
cd ~/c++/sources/chapter_02_01_00/define_01
```

We run the compiler with the -E -P options to output the preprocessing result.

Listing 30. Linux Terminal:

```
g++ -E -P preprocess.hpp -o preprocess.i
```

We load the preprocessing result:

Listing 31. Linux Terminal:

```
code preprocess.i
```

The result of the preprocessing is the following:

Listing 32. `chapter_02_01_00/define_01/preprocess.i`

```
const char* const MESSAGE = "TEST";
const int RESULT = 0;
```

As we can see the compiler has removed the lines starting with # and replaced the definition names with their values everywhere in the source program code.

We compile the test program by running the command:

Listing 33. Linux Terminal

```
g++ -o main main.cpp
```

then we launch it

Listing 34. Linux Terminal

```
./main
```

Example 5. The result of the execution that is displayed on the screen should be the following:

```
TEST
```

We execute the command,

Listing 35. Linux Terminal

```
echo $?
```

which outputs the result returned by the executable.

Example 6. The value should be:

```
0
```

You can experiment with different values after `DEFINED_MESSAGE` or `EXIT_SUCCESS`. If you change the number after `EXIT_SUCCESS` from 0 to 123, recompile, and restart the above program, then the result of `echo $?` will output the new value 123.

Along with the `#define` directive, you can also use the # and ## preprocessor statements.

2.1.1. # returns the name of the directive parameter as a string.

I will show you a short example of how you can use it:

We create a folder in which to put the source code of the program.

Listing 36. Linux Terminal

```
mkdir -p ~/c++/sources/chapter_02_01_00/hashtag_01
```

Then we enter the newly created folder.

Listing 37. Linux Terminal

```
cd ~/c++/sources/chapter_02_01_00/hashtag_01
```

In this folder, we create the files `preprocess.hpp` and `main.cpp`

Listing 38. Linux Terminal

```
code preprocess.hpp main.cpp
```

With the following content:

Listing 39. chapter_02_01_00/hashtag_01/preprocess.hpp

```
#define TEXT(item) #item
```

Listing 40. chapter_02_01_00/hashtag_01/main.cpp

```
#include <iostream>
```

```cpp
#include <limits>
#include <locale>
#include "preprocess.hpp"

int main() {
  unsigned long long unsigned_value_min =
      std::numeric_limits<unsigned long long>::min();
  unsigned long long unsigned_value_max =
      std::numeric_limits<unsigned long long>::max();

  std::cout.imbue(std::locale("en_US.utf8"));

  std::cout << typeid(unsigned_value_max).name() << ":\n";
  std::cout << TEXT(unsigned_value_min) << " = " << unsigned_value_min << "\n";
  std::cout << TEXT(unsigned_value_max) << " = " << unsigned_value_max << "\n";

  signed long long signed_value_min =
      std::numeric_limits<signed long long>::min();
  signed long long signed_value_max =
      std::numeric_limits<signed long long>::max();

  std::cout << std::endl;
  std::cout << typeid(signed_value_max).name() << ":\n";
  std::cout << TEXT(signed_value_min) << " = " << signed_value_min << "\n";
  std::cout << TEXT(signed_value_max) << " = " << signed_value_max << std::endl;

  return 0;
}
```

We compile the test program by running the command:

Listing 41. Linux Terminal

```
sudo apt -y install locales
# Uncomment the en_US.UTF-8 line in /etc/locale.gen
sudo sed -i '/en_US.UTF-8/s/^# //g' /etc/locale.gen
# locale-gen generates locales for all uncommented locales in /etc/locale.gen
sudo locale-gen
# export LANG=en_US.UTF-8

g++ -o main main.cpp
```

then we launch it

Listing 42. Linux Terminal

```
./main
```

Example 7. The result of the execution that is displayed on the screen should be the following:

```
y:
unsigned_value_min = 0
unsigned_value_max = 18,446,744,073,709,551,615

x:
signed_value_min = -9,223,372,036,854,775,808
signed_value_max = 9,223,372,036,854,775,807
```

We execute the command,

Listing 43. Linux Terminal

```
echo $?
```

which outputs the result returned by the executable.

Example 8. The value should be:

```
0
```

2.1.2. ## - concatenates two parameters per definition

I will show you a short example of how you can use it:

We create a folder in which to put the source code of the program.

Listing 44. Linux Terminal

```
mkdir -p ~/c++/sources/chapter_02_01_00/stick_01
```

Then we enter the newly created folder.

Listing 45. Linux Terminal

```
cd ~/c++/sources/chapter_02_01_00/stick_01
```

In this folder, we create the files `preprocess.hpp` and `main.cpp`

Listing 46. Linux Terminal

```
code preprocess.hpp main.cpp
```

With the following content:

Listing 47. `chapter_02_01_00/stick_01/preprocess.hpp`

```cpp
#define STICK(item1, item2) item1##item2

static void print_hello_world() {
  std::string hello_world_message = "Hello, World!";
  STICK(std::c, out) << STICK(hello_world, _message) << STICK(std::en, dl);
}
```

Listing 48. chapter_02_01_00/stick_01/main.cpp

```cpp
#include <iostream>
#include "preprocess.hpp"

int main() {
  print_hello_world();

  return 0;
}
```

We run the compiler with the `-E` `-P` options to
output the preprocessing result.

Listing 49. Linux Terminal:

```
g++ -E -P preprocess.hpp -o preprocess.i
```

We load the preprocessing result:

Listing 50. Linux Terminal:

```
code preprocess.i
```

The result of the preprocessing is the following:

Listing 51. chapter_02_01_00/stick_01/preprocess.i

```cpp
static void print_hello_world() {
  std::string hello_world_message = "Hello, World!";
  std::cout << hello_world_message << std::endl;
}
```

As we can see the compiler has removed the
lines starting with # and replaced the definition
names with their values everywhere in the
source program code.

We compile the test program by running the command:

Listing 52. Linux Terminal

```
g++ -o main main.cpp
```

then we launch it

Listing 53. Linux Terminal

```
./main
```

Example 9. The result of the execution that is displayed on the screen should be the following:

```
Hello, World!
```

We execute the command,

Listing 54. Linux Terminal

```
echo $?
```

which outputs the result returned by the executable.

Example 10. The value should be:

```
0
```

2.2. #elif

The preprocessor conditional statement #elif, in preprocessing, is a complement to the conditional statement #if and checks for another condition if the previous one fails. If the value of the condition is non-zero, the body of the statement is executed, otherwise, it moves to the next #elif, #else, or after #endif when it is the last of the group of conditional statements.

Listing 55. Structure of the conditional operator

```
#if condition1        ①
..                    ②
#elif condition2      ③
..                    ②
#elif condition3      ③
..                    ②
#endif                ④
```

① Start of conditional statement - 0 (false) or non-0 (true).

② Conditional Statement Body A statement body is executed when the condition of the corresponding conditional statement is fulfilled, that is, it is non-zero.

③ The conditional operator in default of the preceding conditions when they are not satisfied.

④ End of preprocessor conditional statement.

I will show you with real examples of **C++** programs what the `#elif` preprocessor command does.

1. We create a folder in which to put the source code of the program.

   Listing 56. Linux Terminal

   ```
   mkdir -p ~/c++/sources/chapter_02_02_00/elif_01
   ```

2. Then we enter the newly created folder.

   Listing 57. Linux Terminal

   ```
   cd ~/c++/sources/chapter_02_02_00/elif_01
   ```

3. In this folder, we create the files `preprocess.hpp` and `main.cpp`

   Listing 58. Linux Terminal

   ```
   code preprocess.hpp main.cpp
   ```

We create program files with the following content:

Listing 59. chapter_02_02_00\elif_01\preprocess.hpp

```
// #define ARRAY_SIZE1 12
#define ARRAY_SIZE2 10

#if defined(ARRAY_SIZE1)
double first_array[ARRAY_SIZE1];
#define ARRAY_SIZE ARRAY_SIZE1
#define ARRAY first_array
#elif defined(ARRAY_SIZE2)
int second_array[ARRAY_SIZE2];
```

```
#define ARRAY_SIZE ARRAY_SIZE2
#define ARRAY second_array
#endif
```

The `main.cpp` file has the following contents:

Listing 60. `chapter_02_02_00\elif_01\main.cpp`

```cpp
#include <iostream>
#include "preprocess.hpp"

int main() {
  for (int index = 0; index < ARRAY_SIZE; ++index) {
    // Set array value:
    ARRAY[index] = index * index;

    // Print array value:
    std::cout << "array[" << index << "] = " << ARRAY[index];
    std::cout << "\t// <-- (" << index << " * " << index << ")";
    std::cout << std::endl;
  }
}
```

In practice, this program uses a loop to fill the array with the squares of its indices `ARRAY[index] = index * index` and output the filled values to the screen.

After we have entered the contents of the files, we perform **preprocessing** by sequentially executing the commands:

1. We enter the folder with the source code of the program.

   Listing 61. Linux Terminal

   ```
   cd ~/c++/sources/chapter_02_02_00/elif_01
   ```

2. We run the compiler with the -E -P options to output the preprocessing result.

Listing 62. Linux Terminal

```
g++ -E -P preprocess.hpp -o preprocess.i
```

We load the preprocessing result:

Listing 63. Linux Terminal:

```
code preprocess.i
```

The result of the preprocessing is the following:

Listing 64. chapter_02_01_00\define_01\preprocess.i

```
int second_array[10];
```

We compile the test program by sequentially executing the commands:

Listing 65. Linux Terminal

```
g++ -o main main.cpp
```

then we launch it

Listing 66. Linux Terminal

```
./main
```

Example 11. The result of the execution that is displayed on the screen should be the following:

```
array[0] = 0    // <-- (0 * 0)
```

```
array[1] = 1     // <-- (1 * 1)
array[2] = 4     // <-- (2 * 2)
array[3] = 9     // <-- (3 * 3)
array[4] = 16    // <-- (4 * 4)
array[5] = 25    // <-- (5 * 5)
array[6] = 36    // <-- (6 * 6)
array[7] = 49    // <-- (7 * 7)
array[8] = 64    // <-- (8 * 8)
array[9] = 81    // <-- (9 * 9)
```

We also display the result returned by the executable file:

Listing 67. Linux Terminal

```
echo $?
```

Example 12. The displayed value must be:

```
0
```

You can experiment - for example with different values after `#define ARRAY_SIZE2` or uncommenting `#define ARRAY_SIZE1`.

2.3. #else

The preprocessor statement #else is an alternative part of the conditional statements #if, #ifdef, or #elif, and its body is executed when the condition is not met.

Listing 68. Structure of the conditional statement #if using the construction #else - "otherwise"

```
#if <condition>              ①
..                           ②
#else                        ③
..                           ②
#endif
```

① Start of conditional statement.

② Conditional statement body.

③ Beginning of the body of the conditional statement when the condition is not met (so-called "else").

Listing 69. Structure of the conditional statement #ifdef using the construct #else - "otherwise"

```
#ifdef <definition name>     ①
..                           ②
#else                        ③
..                           ②
#endif
```

① Start of conditional statement.

② Conditional statement body.

③ Beginning of the body of the conditional

statement when the condition is not met (so-called "else").

I will show you with real examples of **C++** programs what the action of the #else preprocessor command is.

1. We create a folder in which to put the source code of the program.

   Listing 70. Linux Terminal

   ```
   mkdir -p ~/c++/sources/chapter_02_03_00/else_01
   ```

2. Then we enter the newly created folder.

   Listing 71. Linux Terminal

   ```
   cd ~/c++/sources/chapter_02_03_00/else_01
   ```

3. In this folder, we create the files preprocess.hpp and main.cpp

   Listing 72. Linux Terminal

   ```
   code preprocess.hpp main.cpp
   ```

   ## With the following content:

   Listing 73. chapter_02_03_00/else_01/preprocess.hpp

   ```
   // #define ARRAY_SIZE1 12
   #define ARRAY_SIZE2 10

   #if defined(ARRAY_SIZE1)
   double first_array[ARRAY_SIZE1];
   #define ARRAY_SIZE ARRAY_SIZE1
   #define ARRAY first_array
   ```

```
#else
int second_array[ARRAY_SIZE2];
#define ARRAY_SIZE ARRAY_SIZE2
#define ARRAY second_array
#endif
```

The `main.cpp` file has the following contents:

Listing 74. `chapter_02_03_00/else_01/main.cpp`

```cpp
#include <iostream>
#include "preprocess.hpp"

int main() {
  for (int index = 0; index < ARRAY_SIZE; ++index) {
    // Set array value:
    ARRAY[index] = index * index;

    // Print array value:
    std::cout << "array[" << index << "] = " << ARRAY[index];
    std::cout << "\t// <-- (" << index << " * " << index << ")";
    std::cout << std::endl;
  }
}
```

In practice, this program uses a loop to fill the array with the squares of its indices `ARRAY[index] = index * index` and output the filled values to the screen.

After we have entered the contents of the files, we perform **preprocessing** by sequentially executing the commands:

4. We enter the folder with the source code of the program.

Listing 75. Linux Terminal

```
cd ~/c++/sources/chapter_02_03_00/else_01
```

5. We run the compiler with the -E -P options to output the preprocessing result.

Listing 76. Linux Terminal

```
g++ -E -P preprocess.hpp -o preprocess.i
```

We load the preprocessing result:

Listing 77. Linux Terminal:

```
code preprocess.i
```

The result of the preprocessing is the following:

Listing 78. chapter_02_03_00/else_01/preprocess.i

```
int second_array[10];
```

We compile the test program by sequentially executing the commands:

Listing 79. Linux Terminal

```
g++ -o main main.cpp
```

then we launch it

Listing 80. Linux Terminal

```
./main
```

Example 13. The result of the execution that is displayed on the screen should be the following:

```
array[0] = 0     // <-- (0 * 0)
```

```
array[1] = 1    // <-- (1 * 1)
array[2] = 4    // <-- (2 * 2)
array[3] = 9    // <-- (3 * 3)
array[4] = 16   // <-- (4 * 4)
array[5] = 25   // <-- (5 * 5)
array[6] = 36   // <-- (6 * 6)
array[7] = 49   // <-- (7 * 7)
array[8] = 64   // <-- (8 * 8)
array[9] = 81   // <-- (9 * 9)
```

We also display the result returned by the executable file:

Listing 81. Linux Terminal

```
echo $?
```

Example 14. The displayed value must be:

```
0
```

You can experiment - for example with different values after `#define` `ARRAY_SIZE2` or uncommenting `#define ARRAY_SIZE1`.

2.4. #endif

The preprocessor statement #endif ends the conditional statements #if, #ifdef, as well as program blocks for #elif or #else.

Listing 82. In a #if conditional statement structure, the use of the terminating preprocessor statement #endif is mandatory

```
#if <condition>          ①
..                       ②
#endif
```

① Start of conditional statement.

② Conditional operator body.

Listing 83. In a #ifdef conditional statement structure, the use of the terminating preprocessor statement #endif is mandatory

```
#ifdef <definition name>    ①
..                          ②
#endif
```

① Start of conditional statement.

② Conditional operator body.

I will show you with real examples of **C++** programs what the action of the #endif preprocessor command is.

1. We create a folder in which to put the source code of the program.

Listing 84. Linux Terminal

```
mkdir -p ~/c++/sources/chapter_02_04_00/endif_01
```

2. Then we enter the newly created folder.

Listing 85. Linux Terminal

```
cd ~/c++/sources/chapter_02_04_00/endif_01
```

3. In this folder, we create the files preprocess.hpp and main.cpp

Listing 86. Linux Terminal

```
code preprocess.hpp main.cpp
```

With the following content:

Listing 87. chapter_02_04_00/endif_01/preprocess.hpp

```cpp
// #define ARRAY_SIZE1 12
#define ARRAY_SIZE2 10

#if defined(ARRAY_SIZE1)
double first_array[ARRAY_SIZE1];
#define ARRAY_SIZE ARRAY_SIZE1
#define ARRAY first_array
#endif

#if defined(ARRAY_SIZE2)
int second_array[ARRAY_SIZE2];
#define ARRAY_SIZE ARRAY_SIZE2
#define ARRAY second_array
#endif
```

The main.cpp file has the following contents:

Listing 88. chapter_02_04_00/endif_01/main.cpp

```cpp
#include <iostream>
```

```cpp
#include "preprocess.hpp"

int main() {
  for (int index = 0; index < ARRAY_SIZE; ++index) {
    // Set array value:
    ARRAY[index] = index * index;

    // Print array value:
    std::cout << "array[" << index << "] = " << ARRAY[index];
    std::cout << "\t// <-- (" << index << " * " << index << ")";
    std::cout << std::endl;
  }
}
```

In practice, this program uses a loop to fill the array with the squares of its indices `ARRAY[index]` = `index * index` and output the filled values to the screen.

After we have entered the contents of the files, we perform **preprocessing** by sequentially executing the commands:

4. We enter the folder with the source code of the program.

Listing 89. Linux Terminal

```
cd ~/c++/sources/chapter_02_04_00/endif_01
```

5. We run the compiler with the `-E -P` options to output the preprocessing result.

Listing 90. Linux Terminal

```
g++ -E -P preprocess.hpp -o preprocess.i
```

We load the preprocessing result:

Listing 91. Linux Terminal:

```
code preprocess.i
```

The result of the preprocessing is the following:

Listing 92. `chapter_02_04_00/endif_01/preprocess.i`

```
int second_array[10];
```

We compile the test program by sequentially executing the commands:

Listing 93. Linux Terminal

```
g++ -o main main.cpp
```

then we launch it

Listing 94. Linux Terminal

```
./main
```

Example 15. The result of the execution that is displayed on the screen should be the following:

```
array[0] = 0    // <-- (0 * 0)
array[1] = 1    // <-- (1 * 1)
array[2] = 4    // <-- (2 * 2)
array[3] = 9    // <-- (3 * 3)
array[4] = 16   // <-- (4 * 4)
array[5] = 25   // <-- (5 * 5)
array[6] = 36   // <-- (6 * 6)
array[7] = 49   // <-- (7 * 7)
array[8] = 64   // <-- (8 * 8)
array[9] = 81   // <-- (9 * 9)
```

We also display the result returned by the executable file:

Listing 95. Linux Terminal

```
echo $?
```

Example 16. The displayed value must be:

```
0
```

You can experiment - for example with different values after `#define ARRAY_SIZE2` or uncommenting `#define ARRAY_SIZE1`.

2.5. #error

The preprocessor directive #error breaks the compilation and outputs the text after it, as an error message.

Listing 96. Using the #error directive

```
#error <error message>
```

I will show you with real examples of **C++** programs what the action of the #error preprocessor command is.

1. We create a folder in which to put the source code of the program.

   Listing 97. Linux Terminal

   ```
   mkdir -p ~/c++/sources/chapter_02_05_00/error_01
   ```

2. Then we enter the newly created folder.

   Listing 98. Linux Terminal

   ```
   cd ~/c++/sources/chapter_02_05_00/error_01
   ```

3. In this folder, we create the files preprocess.hpp and main.cpp

   Listing 99. Linux Terminal

   ```
   code preprocess.hpp main.cpp
   ```

With the following content:

Listing 100. chapter_02_05_00/error_01/preprocess.hpp

```
#ifdef __unix__
#error This C++ code requires non Unix (Linux) compiler.
#endif
```

The main.cpp file has the following contents:

Listing 101. chapter_02_05_00/error_01/main.cpp

```
#include <cstdlib>
#include "preprocess.hpp"

int main() {
  system("ls");
}
```

This program does not compile under the Unix (Linux) operating system because the execution of the #error statement breaks the compilation process and displays an error message.

4. We enter the folder with the source code of the program.

Listing 102. Linux Terminal

```
cd ~/c++/sources/chapter_02_05_00/error_01
```

5. We compile the test program by running the command:

Listing 103. Linux Terminal

```
g++ -o main main.cpp
```

Example 17. The compilation output displayed on the screen should be as follows:

```
In file included from main.cpp:2:
preprocess.hpp:2:2: error: #error This C++ code requires non Unix (Linux)
compiler.
    2 | #error This C++ code requires non Unix (Linux) compiler.
      |  ^~~~~
```

As we can see the compiler outputs the error message we set with the #error directive and ends the compilation.

We execute the command,

Listing 104. Linux Terminal

```
echo $?
```

which outputs the result returned by the compiler.

Example 18. The value should be:

```
1
```

2.6. #if

The preprocessor conditional statement #if checks a condition and if it is non-zero leaves the program source text found in its body to be compiled. Its body starts at the next line and ends at the #endf preprocessor statement or the next #elif or #else preprocessor statement.

Listing 105. In a #if conditional statement structure, the use of the terminating preprocessor statement #endif is mandatory

```
#if <condition>                    ①
..                                 ②
#endif
```

① Start of conditional statement.

② Conditional statement body.

I will show you real examples of **C++** programs - what the #if preprocessor command does.

1. We create a folder in which to put the source code of the program.

   Listing 106. Linux Terminal

   ```
   mkdir -p ~/c++/sources/chapter_02_06_00/if_01
   ```

2. Then we enter the newly created folder.

Listing 107. Linux Terminal

```
cd ~/c++/sources/chapter_02_06_00/if_01
```

3. In this folder, we create the files preprocess.hpp and main.cpp

Listing 108. Linux Terminal

```
code preprocess.hpp main.cpp
```

With the following content:

Listing 109. chapter_02_06_00/if_01/preprocess.hpp

```
// #define ARRAY_SIZE1 12
#define ARRAY_SIZE2 10

#if defined(ARRAY_SIZE1)
double first_array[ARRAY_SIZE1];
#define ARRAY_SIZE ARRAY_SIZE1
#define ARRAY first_array
#endif

#if defined(ARRAY_SIZE2)
int second_array[ARRAY_SIZE2];
#define ARRAY_SIZE ARRAY_SIZE2
#define ARRAY second_array
#endif
```

The main.cpp file has the following contents:

Listing 110. chapter_02_06_00/if_01/main.cpp

```
#include <iostream>
#include "preprocess.hpp"

int main() {
  for (int index = 0; index < ARRAY_SIZE; ++index) {
    // Set array value:
    ARRAY[index] = index * index;

    // Print array value:
```

```
    std::cout << "array[" << index << "] = " << ARRAY[index];
    std::cout << "\t// <-- (" << index << " * " << index << ")";
    std::cout << std::endl;
  }
}
```

In practice, this program uses a loop to fill the array with the squares of its indices ARRAY[index] = index * index and output the filled values to the screen.

After we have entered the contents of the files, we perform **preprocessing** by sequentially executing the commands:

4. We enter the folder with the source code of the program.

Listing 111. Linux Terminal

```
cd ~/c++/sources/chapter_02_06_00/if_01
```

5. We run the compiler with the -E -P options to output the preprocessing result.

Listing 112. Linux Terminal

```
g++ -E -P preprocess.hpp -o preprocess.i
```

We load the preprocessing result:

Listing 113. Linux Terminal:

```
code preprocess.i
```

The result of the preprocessing is the following:

Listing 114. `chapter_02_06_00/if_01/preprocess.i`

```
int second_array[10];
```

We compile the test program by sequentially executing the commands:

Listing 115. Linux Terminal

```
g++ -o main main.cpp
```

then we launch it

Listing 116. Linux Terminal

```
./main
```

Example 19. The result of the execution that is displayed on the screen should be the following:

```
array[0] = 0     // <-- (0 * 0)
array[1] = 1     // <-- (1 * 1)
array[2] = 4     // <-- (2 * 2)
array[3] = 9     // <-- (3 * 3)
array[4] = 16    // <-- (4 * 4)
array[5] = 25    // <-- (5 * 5)
array[6] = 36    // <-- (6 * 6)
array[7] = 49    // <-- (7 * 7)
array[8] = 64    // <-- (8 * 8)
array[9] = 81    // <-- (9 * 9)
```

We also display the result returned by the executable file:

Listing 117. Linux Terminal

```
echo $?
```

Example 20. The displayed value must be:

```
0
```

You can experiment - for example with different values after `#define` `ARRAY_SIZE2` or uncommenting `#define ARRAY_SIZE1`.

2.7. #ifdef

The preprocessor conditional statement `#ifdef` checks whether a given name is defined.

Listing 118. In a #ifdef conditional statement structure, the use of the terminating preprocessor statement #endif is mandatory

```
#ifdef <name>    ①
..               ②
#endif
```

① Start of conditional statement.

② Conditional operator body.

I will show you real examples of **C++** programs - what the `#ifdef` preprocessor command does.

1. We create a folder in which to put the source code of the program.

   Listing 119. Linux Terminal

   ```
   mkdir -p ~/c++/sources/chapter_02_07_00/ifdef_01
   ```

2. Then we enter the newly created folder.

   Listing 120. Linux Terminal

   ```
   cd ~/c++/sources/chapter_02_07_00/ifdef_01
   ```

3. In this folder, we create the files `preprocess.hpp` and `main.cpp`

Listing 121. Linux Terminal

```
code preprocess.hpp main.cpp
```

With the following content:

Listing 122. `chapter_02_07_00/ifdef_01/preprocess.hpp`

```
// #define ARRAY_SIZE1 12
#define ARRAY_SIZE2 10

#ifdef ARRAY_SIZE1
double first_array[ARRAY_SIZE1];
#define ARRAY_SIZE ARRAY_SIZE1
#define ARRAY first_array
#endif

#if defined(ARRAY_SIZE2)
int second_array[ARRAY_SIZE2];
#define ARRAY_SIZE ARRAY_SIZE2
#define ARRAY second_array
#endif
```

The `main.cpp` file has the following contents:

Listing 123. `chapter_02_07_00/ifdef_01/main.cpp`

```cpp
#include <iostream>
#include "preprocess.hpp"

int main() {
  for (int index = 0; index < ARRAY_SIZE; ++index) {
    // Set array value:
    ARRAY[index] = index * index;

    // Print array value:
    std::cout << "array[" << index << "] = " << ARRAY[index];
    std::cout << "\t// <-- (" << index << " * " << index << ")";
    std::cout << std::endl;
  }
}
```

In practice, this program uses a loop to fill the array with the squares of its indices

`ARRAY[index] = index * index` and output the filled values to the screen.

After we have entered the contents of the files, we perform **preprocessing** by sequentially executing the commands:

4. We enter the folder with the source code of the program.

Listing 124. Linux Terminal

```
cd ~/c++/sources/chapter_02_07_00/ifdef_01
```

5. We run the compiler with the `-E -P` options to output the preprocessing result.

Listing 125. Linux Terminal

```
g++ -E -P preprocess.hpp -o preprocess.i
```

We load the preprocessing result:

Listing 126. Linux Terminal:

```
code preprocess.i
```

The result of the preprocessing is the following:

Listing 127. chapter_02_07_00/ifdef_01/preprocess.i

```
int second_array[10];
```

We compile the test program by executing the command:

Listing 128. Linux Terminal

```
g++ -o main main.cpp
```

then we launch it

Listing 129. Linux Terminal

```
./main
```

Example 21. The result of the execution that is displayed on the screen should be the following:

```
array[0] = 0     // <-- (0 * 0)
array[1] = 1     // <-- (1 * 1)
array[2] = 4     // <-- (2 * 2)
array[3] = 9     // <-- (3 * 3)
array[4] = 16    // <-- (4 * 4)
array[5] = 25    // <-- (5 * 5)
array[6] = 36    // <-- (6 * 6)
array[7] = 49    // <-- (7 * 7)
array[8] = 64    // <-- (8 * 8)
array[9] = 81    // <-- (9 * 9)
```

We also display the result returned by the executable file:

Listing 130. Linux Terminal

```
echo $?
```

Example 22. The displayed value must be:

```
0
```

You can experiment - for example with different

values after `#define` `ARRAY_SIZE2` or uncommenting `#define ARRAY_SIZE1`.

2.8. #ifndef

The preprocessor conditional statement `#ifndef` checks whether a specified name is undefined.

Listing 131. In a `#ifndef` conditional statement structure, the use of the terminating preprocessor statement `#endif` is mandatory

```
#ifndef <name>    ①
..                ②
#endif
```

① Start of conditional statement.

② Conditional statement body.

I will show you examples of **C++** programs - what the `#ifndef` preprocessor command does.

1. We create a folder in which to put the source code of the program.

   Listing 132. Linux Terminal

   ```
   mkdir -p ~/c++/sources/chapter_02_08_00/ifndef_01
   ```

2. Then we enter the newly created folder.

   Listing 133. Linux Terminal

   ```
   cd ~/c++/sources/chapter_02_08_00/ifndef_01
   ```

3. In this folder, we create the files `preprocess.hpp` and `main.cpp`

Listing 134. Linux Terminal

```
code preprocess.hpp main.cpp
```

With the following content:

Listing 135. chapter_02_08_00/ifndef_01/preprocess.hpp

```
// #define ARRAY_SIZE1 12
#define ARRAY_SIZE2 10

#ifndef ARRAY_SIZE2
double first_array[ARRAY_SIZE1];
#define ARRAY_SIZE ARRAY_SIZE1
#define ARRAY first_array
#endif

#ifndef ARRAY_SIZE1
int second_array[ARRAY_SIZE2];
#define ARRAY_SIZE ARRAY_SIZE2
#define ARRAY second_array
#endif
```

The main.cpp file has the following contents:

Listing 136. chapter_02_08_00/ifndef_01/main.cpp

```
#include <iostream>
#include "preprocess.hpp"

int main() {
  for (int index = 0; index < ARRAY_SIZE; ++index) {
    // Set array value:
    ARRAY[index] = index * index;

    // Print array value:
    std::cout << "array[" << index << "] = " << ARRAY[index];
    std::cout << "\t// <-- (" << index << " * " << index << ")";
    std::cout << std::endl;
  }
}
```

In practice, this program uses a loop to fill the array with the squares of its indices

`ARRAY[index] = index * index` and output the filled values to the screen.

After we have entered the contents of the files, we perform **preprocessing** by sequentially executing the commands:

4. We enter the folder with the source code of the program.

Listing 137. Linux Terminal

```
cd ~/c++/sources/chapter_02_08_00/ifndef_01
```

5. We run the compiler with the `-E -P` options to output the preprocessing result.

Listing 138. Linux Terminal

```
g++ -E -P preprocess.hpp -o preprocess.i
```

We load the preprocessing result:

Listing 139. Linux Terminal:

```
code preprocess.i
```

The result of the preprocessing is the following:

Listing 140. chapter_02_08_00/ifndef_01/preprocess.i

```
int second_array[10];
```

We compile the test program by sequentially executing the commands:

Listing 141. Linux Terminal

```
g++ -o main main.cpp
```

then we launch it

Listing 142. Linux Terminal

```
./main
```

Example 23. The result of the execution that is displayed on the screen should be the following:

```
array[0] = 0     // <-- (0 * 0)
array[1] = 1     // <-- (1 * 1)
array[2] = 4     // <-- (2 * 2)
array[3] = 9     // <-- (3 * 3)
array[4] = 16    // <-- (4 * 4)
array[5] = 25    // <-- (5 * 5)
array[6] = 36    // <-- (6 * 6)
array[7] = 49    // <-- (7 * 7)
array[8] = 64    // <-- (8 * 8)
array[9] = 81    // <-- (9 * 9)
```

We also display the result returned by the executable file:

Listing 143. Linux Terminal

```
echo $?
```

Example 24. The displayed value must be:

```
0
```

You can experiment - for example with different

values after `#define` `ARRAY_SIZE2` or uncommenting `#define ARRAY_SIZE1`.

2.9. #include

The preprocessor conditional statement `#include` inserts the contents of a file specified after it in angle brackets or quotation marks.

Listing 144. Using the `#include` preprocessor statement to insert content

```
#include <file name>          ①
#include "file name"          ②
```

① Inserting content from the C/C++ system libraries.

② Insert content from a path relative to the current source file.

I will show you real examples of **C++** programs - what the `#include` preprocessor command does.

1. We create a folder in which to put the source code of the program.

   Listing 145. Linux Terminal

   ```
   mkdir -p ~/c++/sources/chapter_02_09_00/include_01
   ```

2. Then we enter the newly created folder.

   Listing 146. Linux Terminal

   ```
   cd ~/c++/sources/chapter_02_09_00/include_01
   ```

3. In this folder we create the files

my_function.hpp, my_function.cpp, preprocess.hpp and main.cpp

Listing 147. Linux Terminal

```
code my_function.hpp my_function.cpp preprocess.hpp main.cpp
```

With the following content:

Listing 148. `chapter_02_09_00/include_01/my_function.hpp`

```cpp
#ifndef PRINT_HELLO_WORLD_HPP  // Header guard
#define PRINT_HELLO_WORLD_HPP

void print_hello_world();

#endif  // PRINT_HELLO_WORLD_HPP
```

Listing 149. `chapter_02_09_00/include_01/my_function.cpp`

```cpp
#include "my_function.hpp"
#include <iostream>

void print_hello_world() {
  std::cout << "Hello, World!" << std::endl;
}
```

Listing 150. `chapter_02_09_00/include_01/preprocess.hpp`

```cpp
#include "my_function.hpp"
```

The `main.cpp` file has the following contents:

Listing 151. `chapter_02_09_00/include_01/main.cpp`

```cpp
#include "preprocess.hpp"

int main() {
  print_hello_world();
}
```

In practice, this program implements the print_hello_world function, which is declared in the my_function.hpp file and defined in the my_function.cpp file.

After we have entered the contents of the files, we perform **preprocessing** by sequentially executing the commands:

4. We enter the folder with the source code of the program.

Listing 152. Linux Terminal

```
cd ~/c++/sources/chapter_02_09_00/include_01
```

5. We run the compiler with the -E -P options to output the preprocessing result.

Listing 153. Linux Terminal

```
g++ -E -P preprocess.hpp -o preprocess.i
```

We load the preprocessing result:

Listing 154. Linux Terminal:

```
code preprocess.i
```

The result of the preprocessing is the following:

Listing 155. chapter_02_09_00/include_01/preprocess.i

```
void print_hello_world();
```

We compile the test program by sequentially executing the commands:

Listing 156. Linux Terminal

```
g++ -o main **.c*
```

then we launch it

Listing 157. Linux Terminal

```
./main
```

Example 25. The result of the execution that is displayed on the screen should be the following:

```
Hello, World!
```

We also display the result returned by the executable file:

Listing 158. Linux Terminal

```
echo $?
```

Example 26. The displayed value must be:

```
0
```

2.10. #line

The `#line` preprocessor operator specifies the next line number of the source code as its first parameter and the file name as an optional second parameter.

 It is often used by the compiler preprocessor itself when including header files, via the `#include` preprocessor directive, to correctly output error numbers and filenames.

Listing 159. Using the `#line` preprocessor statement to override line numbering

```
#line <line number> "<file name>"        ①
int number="23";                          ②
```

① The principle use of the `#line` preprocessor operator.

② A line containing an error in the **C++** code.

I will show you real examples of **C++** programs - what the `#line` preprocessor command does.

1. We create a folder in which to put the source code of the program.

Listing 160. Linux Terminal

```
mkdir -p ~/c++/sources/chapter_02_10_00/line_01
```

2. Then we enter the newly created folder.

Listing 161. Linux Terminal

```
cd ~/c++/sources/chapter_02_10_00/line_01
```

3. In this folder, we create the files `preprocess.hpp` and `main.cpp`

Listing 162. Linux Terminal

```
code preprocess.hpp main.cpp
```

With the following content:

Listing 163. `chapter_02_10_00/line_01/preprocess.hpp`

```
#line 55 "preprocess header"
int number = "23";
```

The `main.cpp` file has the following contents:

Listing 164. `chapter_02_10_00/line_01/main.cpp`

```
#include "preprocess.hpp"

int main() {}
```

This program does not compile because there is an error in the program source code.

4. We enter the folder with the source code of the program.

Listing 165. Linux Terminal

```
cd ~/c++/sources/chapter_02_10_00/line_01
```

5. We compile the test program by running the command:

Listing 166. Linux Terminal

```
g++ -o main main.cpp
```

Example 27. The compilation output displayed on the screen should be as follows:

```
In file included from main.cpp:1:
preprocess header:55:14: error: invalid conversion from 'const char*' to
'int' [-fpermissive]
```

As we can see, the compiler outputs the error message, with the line number and file name that we set with the #line preprocessor statement.

We execute the command,

Listing 167. Linux Terminal

```
echo $?
```

which outputs the result returned by the compiler.

Example 28. The value should be:

```
1
```

2.11. #pragma

The #pragma preprocessor statement sets various settings for how **C**++ source code will be compiled.

Listing 168. Using the #pragma preprocessor statement

```
#pragma <command>
```

We will only look at the main commands to the #pragma preprocessor operator:

Listing 169. Using the #pragma preprocessor statement to limit loading a file only once - used for files loaded with the #include preprocessor statement

```
#pragma once
```

Listing 170. Using the #pragma preprocessor statement to wrap variables, structs, and classes. Aligns the size of variables and constants to a specified number of bytes. Usually, by default, alignment is set to the number of bytes characteristic of the respective processor architecture - for example, 8 bytes for 64-bit, and 4 bytes for 32-bit. When we specify the alignment to be 1 byte, then the element takes up minimal space, but at the same time, access to it is slightly less efficient.

```
#pragma pack(push, 1)
#pragma pack(pop)
```

Listing 171. Using the #pragma preprocessor statement to select a specific static library to link to the executable.

```
#pragma comment(lib, "ws2_32.lib")
#pragma comment(lib, "WSock32.Lib")
```

Listing 172. Using the `#pragma` *preprocessor statement to temporarily un-define a preprocessor directive.*

```
#pragma push_macro("min")
#pragma pop_macro("min")
```

Listing 173. Using the `#pragma` *preprocessor statement to output a message.*

```
#pragma message("This C++ code prefers the Linux compiler.")
```

There are also additional commands to the `#pragma` preprocessor operator that I have practically never had to use in the projects I have worked on over the years. Such as turning off some compilation remarks, and instead of using them, it is better to fix the program code itself or use a compiler command line option.

2.11.1. #pragma once

I will show you with real examples of **C++** programs what the preprocessor command `#pragma once` does.

1. We create a folder in which to put the source code of the program.

    Listing 174. Linux Terminal

    ```
    mkdir -p ~/c++/sources/chapter_02_11_00/once_01
    ```

1. Then we enter the newly created folder.

    Listing 175. Linux Terminal

    ```
    cd ~/c++/sources/chapter_02_11_00/once_01
    ```

1. In this folder we create the files `my_function.hpp`, `my_function.cpp`, `preprocess.hpp` and `main.cpp`

    Listing 176. Linux Terminal

    ```
    code my_function.hpp my_function.cpp preprocess.hpp main.cpp
    ```

    ## With the following content:

    Listing 177. chapter_02_11_00/once_01/my_function.hpp

    ```
    #pragma once  // Header guard

    void print_hello_world();
    ```

Listing 178. chapter_02_11_00/once_01/my_function.cpp

```cpp
#include "my_function.hpp"
#include <iostream>

void print_hello_world() {
  std::cout << "Hello, World!" << std::endl;
}
```

Listing 179. chapter_02_11_00/once_01/preprocess.hpp

```cpp
#include "my_function.hpp"
```

The main.cpp file has the following contents:

Listing 180. chapter_02_11_00/once_01/main.cpp

```cpp
#include "preprocess.hpp"

int main() {
  print_hello_world();
}
```

In practice, this program implements the function print_hello_world, which is declared in the file my_function.hpp and defined in the file my_function.cpp.

We compile the test program by sequentially executing the commands:

Listing 181. Linux Terminal

```
g++ -o main **.c*
```

then we launch it

Listing 182. Linux Terminal

```
./main
```

Example 29. The result of the execution that is displayed on the screen should be the following:

```
Hello, World!
```

We also display the result returned by the executable file:

Listing 183. Linux Terminal

```
echo $?
```

Example 30. The displayed value must be:

```
0
```

2.11.2. #pragma pack

I will show you with real examples of **C++** programs what the #pragma pack preprocessor command does.

1. We create a folder in which to put the source code of the program.

Listing 184. Linux Terminal

```
mkdir -p ~/c++/sources/chapter_02_11_00/pack_01
```

1. Then we enter the newly created folder.

Listing 185. Linux Terminal

```
cd ~/c++/sources/chapter_02_11_00/pack_01
```

1. In this folder, we create the main.cpp file

Listing 186. Linux Terminal

```
code main.cpp
```

With the following content:

Listing 187. chapter_02_11_00/pack_01/main.cpp

```cpp
#include <iostream>

#pragma pack(push, 1)
struct Packed {
  unsigned char one_byte;
  unsigned long long int eight_bytes;
  unsigned short two_bytes;
  unsigned short two_bytes_again;
};
```

```cpp
#pragma pack(pop)

struct UnPacked {
  unsigned char one_byte;
  unsigned long long int eight_bytes;
  unsigned short two_bytes;
  unsigned short two_bytes_again;
};

#pragma pack(push, 2)
struct UnPacked_2_Bytes_Aligned {
  unsigned char one_byte;
  unsigned long long int eight_bytes;
  unsigned short two_bytes;
  unsigned short two_bytes_again;
};
#pragma pack(pop)

int main() {
  std::cout << "sizeof(Packed) = " << sizeof(Packed) << " bytes\n";
  std::cout << "offsetof(Packed, one_byte) = " << offsetof(Packed, one_byte)
            << "\n";
  std::cout << "offsetof(Packed, eight_bytes) = "
            << offsetof(Packed, eight_bytes) << "\n";
  std::cout << "offsetof(Packed, two_bytes) = " << offsetof(Packed, two_bytes)
            << "\n";
  std::cout << "offsetof(Packed, two_bytes_again) = "
            << offsetof(Packed, two_bytes_again) << "\n\n";

  std::cout << "sizeof(UnPacked) = " << sizeof(UnPacked) << " bytes\n";
  std::cout << "offsetof(UnPacked, one_byte) = " << offsetof(UnPacked,
one_byte)
            << "\n";
  std::cout << "offsetof(UnPacked, eight_bytes) = "
            << offsetof(UnPacked, eight_bytes) << "\n";
  std::cout << "offsetof(UnPacked, two_bytes) = "
            << offsetof(UnPacked, two_bytes) << "\n";
  std::cout << "offsetof(UnPacked, two_bytes_again) = "
            << offsetof(UnPacked, two_bytes_again) << "\n\n";

  std::cout << "sizeof(UnPacked_2_Bytes_Aligned) = "
            << sizeof(UnPacked_2_Bytes_Aligned) << " bytes\n";
  std::cout << "offsetof(UnPacked_2_Bytes_Aligned, one_byte) = "
            << offsetof(UnPacked_2_Bytes_Aligned, one_byte) << "\n";
  std::cout << "offsetof(UnPacked_2_Bytes_Aligned, eight_bytes) = "
            << offsetof(UnPacked_2_Bytes_Aligned, eight_bytes) << "\n";
  std::cout << "offsetof(UnPacked_2_Bytes_Aligned, two_bytes) = "
            << offsetof(UnPacked_2_Bytes_Aligned, two_bytes) << "\n";
  std::cout << "offsetof(UnPacked_2_Bytes_Aligned, two_bytes_again) = "
            << offsetof(UnPacked_2_Bytes_Aligned, two_bytes_again) << std
::endl;
```

```
}
```

In practice, this program compares the sizes of different structures with fields of the same size and the offset of each field relative to the beginning of the corresponding structure at different values of the number of bytes to which the compiler aligns the sizes of the structures and their fields. The situation is similar when using classes instead of structs, but then when inheriting from the base class(es) there is additional information about the base class(es) as well.

We compile the test program by sequentially executing the commands:

Listing 188. Linux Terminal

```
g++ -o main main.cpp
```

then we launch it

Listing 189. Linux Terminal

```
./main
```

Example 31. The result of the execution that is displayed on the screen should be the following:

```
sizeof(Packed) = 13 bytes
offsetof(Packed, one_byte) = 0
offsetof(Packed, eight_bytes) = 1
offsetof(Packed, two_bytes) = 9
offsetof(Packed, two_bytes_again) = 11
```

```
sizeof(UnPacked) = 24 bytes
offsetof(UnPacked, one_byte) = 0
offsetof(UnPacked, eight_bytes) = 8
offsetof(UnPacked, two_bytes) = 16
offsetof(UnPacked, two_bytes_again) = 18

sizeof(UnPacked_2_Bytes_Aligned) = 14 bytes
offsetof(UnPacked_2_Bytes_Aligned, one_byte) = 0
offsetof(UnPacked_2_Bytes_Aligned, eight_bytes) = 2
offsetof(UnPacked_2_Bytes_Aligned, two_bytes) = 10
offsetof(UnPacked_2_Bytes_Aligned, two_bytes_again) = 12
```

We also display the result returned by the executable file:

Listing 190. Linux Terminal

```
echo $?
```

Example 32. The displayed value must be:

```
0
```

2.11.3. #pragma comment

I will show you with real examples of **C++** programs what the preprocessor command `#pragma comment` does.

1. We create a folder in which to put the source code of the program.

   Listing 191. Linux Terminal

   ```
   mkdir -p ~/c++/sources/chapter_02_11_00/comment_01
   ```

1. Then we enter the newly created folder.

   Listing 192. Linux Terminal

   ```
   cd ~/c++/sources/chapter_02_11_00/comment_01
   ```

1. In this folder, we create the `main.cpp` file

   Listing 193. Linux Terminal

   ```
   code main.cpp
   ```

   ## With the following content:

   Listing 194. chapter_02_11_00/comment_01/main.cpp

   ```cpp
   // Next line does not working in Unix (Linux) "g++" compiler.
   // #pragma comment(lib, "uuid")
   // In such case just use the "-luuid" option at the end of the "g++" compiler
   // command line.

   #include <uuid/uuid.h>
   #include <cstdlib>
   #include <iostream>
   #include <string>
   ```

```
std::string newUUID() {
  uuid_t uuid;
  char result[37];

  uuid_generate_random(uuid);
  uuid_unparse(uuid, result);

  return std::string(result);
}

int main() {
  std::cout << "New UUID: " << newUUID() << std::endl;

  return EXIT_SUCCESS;
}
```

In practice, this program generates an unique Universally Unique IDentifier (UUID).

We compile the test program by sequentially executing the commands:

Listing 195. Linux Terminal

```
# Installing the "uuid" library
sudo apt -y install uuid-dev

# Compiling the "main.cpp" source file with the external "uuid" library.
g++ -Werror=unknown-pragmas -o main main.cpp -luuid
```

then we launch it

Listing 196. Linux Terminal

```
./main
```

Example 33. The result of the execution that is displayed on the screen should be something like the following:

```
New UUID: 2d84d6d1-5351-4959-9d9a-a8f3c7feef43
```

We also display the result returned by the executable file:

Listing 197. Linux Terminal

```
echo $?
```

Example 34. The displayed value must be:

```
0
```

2.11.4. #pragma push_macro and pop_macro

I will show you with real examples of **C++** programs what the preprocessor commands `#pragma push_macro` and `#pragma pop_macro` do.

1. We create a folder in which to put the source code of the program.

   Listing 198. Linux Terminal

   ```
   mkdir -p ~/c++/sources/chapter_02_11_00/macro_01
   ```

1. Then we enter the newly created folder.

   Listing 199. Linux Terminal

   ```
   cd ~/c++/sources/chapter_02_11_00/macro_01
   ```

1. In this folder, we create the `main.cpp` file

   Listing 200. Linux Terminal

   ```
   code main.cpp
   ```

   ## With the following content:

   Listing 201. chapter_02_11_00/macro_01/main.cpp

   ```cpp
   #include <sys/param.h>  // MIN
   #include <cstdlib>      // EXIT_SUCCESS
   #include <iostream>     // std::cout, <<, std::endl

   #pragma push_macro("MIN")
   #undef MIN
   int MIN(int first, int second) {
   ```

```cpp
  int result = first < second ? first : second;

  std::cout << "minimum of " << first << " and " << second << " is " << result
            << std::endl;

  return result;
}
#pragma pop_macro("MIN")

int main() {
  int first = 10;
  int second = 20;

  std::cout << "Predefined `MIN` macro result: " << MIN(first, second)
            << "\n\n";

#pragma push_macro("MIN")
#undef MIN
  std::cout << "Our `MIN` function result: "
            << "\n";
  MIN(first, second);
#pragma pop_macro("MIN")

  return EXIT_SUCCESS;
}
```

This program compares two values and returns the smaller of them.

We compile the test program by sequentially executing the commands:

Listing 202. Linux Terminal

```
g++ -o main main.cpp
```

then we launch it

Listing 203. Linux Terminal

```
./main
```

Example 35. The result of the execution that is displayed on the screen should be the following:

```
Predefined `MIN` macro result: 10

Our `MIN` function result:
minimum of 10 and 20 is 10
```

We also display the result returned by the executable file:

Listing 204. Linux Terminal

```
echo $?
```

Example 36. The displayed value must be:

```
0
```

2.11.5. #pragma message

The preprocessor directive `#pragma message` outputs the text after it, as a warning during the compilation of the source code of a **C++** program.

Listing 205. Using the `#pragma message` directive

```
#pragma message("<warning>")
```

I will show you with real examples of **C++** programs what the preprocessor command `#pragma message` does.

1. We create a folder in which to put the source code of the program.

   Listing 206. Linux Terminal

   ```
   mkdir -p ~/c++/sources/chapter_02_11_00/message_01
   ```

2. Then we enter the newly created folder.

   Listing 207. Linux Terminal

   ```
   cd ~/c++/sources/chapter_02_11_00/message_01
   ```

3. In this folder, we create the files `preprocess.hpp` and `main.cpp`

   Listing 208. Linux Terminal

   ```
   code preprocess.hpp main.cpp
   ```

With the following content:

Listing 209. chapter_02_11_00/message_01/preprocess.hpp

```
#define TEXT(item) #item
#define TO_TEXT(item) TEXT(item)

#ifndef _WIN32
#pragma message("(" __FILE__ ", " TO_TEXT( \
    __LINE__) "): This C++ code prefers the Windows compiler.")
#endif
```

The `main.cpp` file has the following contents:

Listing 210. chapter_02_13_00/warning_01/main.cpp

```
#include <cstdlib>
#include "preprocess.hpp"

int main() {
  system("dir");
}
```

This program compiles and outputs a warning message.

4. We enter the folder with the source code of the program.

Listing 211. Linux Terminal

```
cd ~/c++/sources/chapter_02_11_00/message_01
```

5. We compile the test program by running the command:

Listing 212. Linux Terminal

```
g++ -o main main.cpp
```

Example 37. The compilation output displayed on the screen should be as follows:

```
In file included from main.cpp:2:
preprocess.hpp:6:63: note: '#pragma message: (preprocess.hpp, 6): This C++
code prefers the Windows compiler.'
    6 |     __LINE__) "): This C++ code prefers the Windows compiler.")
      |                                                               ^
```

As we can see the compiler outputs the message we set with the #warning directive.

We execute the command,

Listing 213. Linux Terminal

```
echo $?
```

which outputs the result returned by the compiler.

Example 38. The value should be:

```
0
```

2.12. #undef

The #undef preprocessor statement removes a definition created by the #define preprocessor statement.

I will show you with real examples of **C++** programs what the #undef preprocessor operator does.

1. We create a folder in which to put the source code of the program.

   Listing 214. Linux Terminal

   ```
   mkdir -p ~/c++/sources/chapter_02_12_00/undef_01
   ```

2. Then we enter the newly created folder.

   Listing 215. Linux Terminal

   ```
   cd ~/c++/sources/chapter_02_12_00/undef_01
   ```

3. In this folder, we create the main.cpp file

   Listing 216. Linux Terminal

   ```
   code main.cpp
   ```

   ## With the following content:

   Listing 217. chapter_02_12_00/undef_01/main.cpp

   ```cpp
   #include <sys/param.h>  // MIN
   #include <cstdlib>      // EXIT_SUCCESS
   ```

```cpp
#include <iostream>    // std::cout, <<, std::endl

#undef MIN
int MIN(int first, int second) {
  int result = first < second ? first : second;

  std::cout << "minimum of " << first << " and " << second << " is " << result
            << std::endl;

  return result;
}

int main() {
  int first = 10;
  int second = 20;

  std::cout << "Our `MIN` function result: "
            << "\n";
  MIN(first, second);

  return EXIT_SUCCESS;
}
```

This program compares two values and returns the smaller of them by overriding the MIN definition loaded by using the sys/param.h file and using our function of the same name. This is a way of overriding definitions that conflict with the **C++** functions we created or other definitions.

We compile the test program by sequentially executing the commands:

Listing 218. Linux Terminal

```
g++ -o main main.cpp
```

then we launch it

Listing 219. Linux Terminal

```
./main
```

Example 39. The result of the execution that is displayed on the screen should be the following:

```
Our `MIN` function result:
minimum of 10 and 20 is 10
```

We also display the result returned by the executable file:

Listing 220. Linux Terminal

```
echo $?
```

Example 40. The displayed value must be:

```
0
```

Chapter 3. Description of the program code

3.1. define_01/preprocess.hpp

Listing 221.
~/c++/sources/chapter_02_01_00/define_01/preprocess.hpp

```cpp
#define DEFINED_MESSAGE "TEST"
#define EXIT_SUCCESS 0

const char* const MESSAGE = DEFINED_MESSAGE;
const int RESULT = EXIT_SUCCESS;
```

We define text

Listing 222. preprocess.hpp#1

```cpp
#define DEFINED_MESSAGE "TEST"
```

We define a number

Listing 223. preprocess.hpp#2

```cpp
#define EXIT_SUCCESS 0
```

We use the defined text

Listing 224. preprocess.hpp#4

```cpp
const char* const MESSAGE = DEFINED_MESSAGE;
```

We use the defined number

Listing 225. `preprocess.hpp#5`

```cpp
const int RESULT = EXIT_SUCCESS;
```

3.2. define_01/main.cpp

Listing 226.
`~/c++/sources/chapter_02_01_00/define_01/main.cpp`

```cpp
#include <iostream>
#include "preprocess.hpp"

int main() {
  std::cout << MESSAGE << std::endl;

  return RESULT;
}
```

We use the defined text.

Listing 227. `main.cpp#5`

```cpp
std::cout << MESSAGE << std::endl;
```

We use the defined number.

Listing 228. `main.cpp#7`

```cpp
return RESULT;
```

3.3. elif_01/preprocess.hpp

Listing 229.
`~/c++/sources/chapter_02_02_00/elif_01/preprocess.hpp`

```
// #define ARRAY_SIZE1 12
#define ARRAY_SIZE2 10

#if defined(ARRAY_SIZE1)
double first_array[ARRAY_SIZE1];
#define ARRAY_SIZE ARRAY_SIZE1
#define ARRAY first_array
#elif defined(ARRAY_SIZE2)
int second_array[ARRAY_SIZE2];
#define ARRAY_SIZE ARRAY_SIZE2
#define ARRAY second_array
#endif
```

Listing 230. `preprocess.hpp#1`

```
// #define ARRAY_SIZE1 12
```

We set an array size definition that we have commented out so that it is not involved in compiling the program.

Listing 231. `preprocess.hpp#2`

```
#define ARRAY_SIZE2 10
```

We set one more array size definition that will be used when compiling the program.

Listing 232. `preprocess.hpp#4`

```
#if defined(ARRAY_SIZE1)
```

Start of conditional preprocessor statement `#if`. The expression `defined(ARRAY_SIZE1)` checks if we have a preprocessor definition `ARRAY_SIZE1` defined. In this particular case, we don't because our definition is not processed by the compiler because we marked it as a comment. The preprocessor function `defined` returns `1` or `0` depending on whether the name in the parentheses is defined or not, in which case it returns `0`.

Listing 233. `preprocess.hpp#5`

```
double first_array[ARRAY_SIZE1];
```

This is the first line of the body of the conditional `#if` preprocessor statement. Here we define an array `first_array` of real numbers with double precision `double` and size `ARRAY_SIZE1`. In this particular case, this part of the code will not be compiled because the condition of the `#if` preprocessor statement is not met.

Listing 234. `preprocess.hpp#6`

```
#define ARRAY_SIZE ARRAY_SIZE1
```

This is the second line of the body of the conditional #if preprocessor statement. Here we set the size ARRAY_SIZE of the array that will be used in the program. This part of the code will not be compiled because the condition of the preprocessor #if statement is not met.

Listing 235. `preprocess.hpp#7`

```
#define ARRAY first_array
```

This is the third line of the body of the conditional #if preprocessor statement. Here we name the array that will be used in the program as ARRAY. This part of the code will also not be compiled because the condition of the preprocessor #if statement is not met.

Listing 236. `preprocess.hpp#8`

```
#elif defined(ARRAY_SIZE2)
```

This is the first alternative conditional operator #elif whose condition is checked when the condition of the #if operator is not met. Here we check if the ARRAY_SIZE2 preprocessor definition is set using the `defined` preprocessor function. This part of the code will be compiled because the condition of the preprocessor statement `#elif` is met, ie. `ARRAY_SIZE2` is defined by the preprocessor somewhere in the code before the current check.

Listing 237. `preprocess.hpp#9`

```
int second_array[ARRAY_SIZE2];
```

This is the first line of the body of the alternative conditional preprocessor `#elif`. Here we define an array `second_array` of integers `int` and size `ARRAY_SIZE2`. In this particular case, this part of the code will be compiled because the condition of the preprocessor operator `#elif` is met.

Listing 238. `preprocess.hpp#10`

```
#define ARRAY_SIZE ARRAY_SIZE2
```

This is the second line of the body of the alternative conditional preprocessor `#elif`. Here we set the size `ARRAY_SIZE` of the array that will be used in the program. This part of the code will be compiled because the condition of the preprocessor operator `#elif` is met.

Listing 239. `preprocess.hpp#11`

```
#define ARRAY second_array
```

This is the third line of the body of the alternative conditional preprocessor `#elif`. Here we name the array that will be used in the program as ARRAY. This part of the code will also be compiled because the condition of the preprocessor statement `#elif` is met.

Listing 240. `preprocess.hpp#12`

```
#endif
```

The preprocessor statement `#endif` specifies the end of one of the conditional preprocessor statements `#if` or `#ifdef`. In this case, it also specifies the end of the body of the alternative conditional preprocessor `#elif`.

3.4. elif_01/main.cpp

Listing 241.
~/c++/sources/chapter_02_02_00/elif_01/main.cpp

```cpp
#include <iostream>
#include "preprocess.hpp"

int main() {
  for (int index = 0; index < ARRAY_SIZE; ++index) {
    // Set array value:
    ARRAY[index] = index * index;

    // Print array value:
    std::cout << "array[" << index << "] = " << ARRAY[index];
    std::cout << "\t// <-- (" << index << " * " << index << ")";
    std::cout << std::endl;
  }
}
```

In practice, this program uses a loop to fill the array with the squares of its indices `ARRAY[index] = index * index` and output the filled values to the screen.

Let us consider the meaning of each line of it.

Listing 242.
~/c++/sources/chapter_02_02_00/elif_01/main.cpp#1

```cpp
#include <iostream>
```

This line uses the `#include` preprocessor directive to load the stream handler definitions from the `iostream` file containing their descriptions. In our case, we use the `std::cout`, `<<`, and `std::endl` operators, with the help of which we display messages on the screen in the text console from which we run the program. The `iostream` library is part of the **Standard Template Library (STL)** of **C++**.

Listing 243.
~/c++/sources/chapter_02_02_00/elif_01/main.cpp#2

```
#include "preprocess.hpp"
```

This line uses the `#include` preprocessor directive to load the definitions we've specified to use in our program from the `preprocess.hpp` file containing their descriptions. In our case, we use the preprocessor definitions `ARRAY_SIZE` and `ARRAY`. As we can see they hide the specific sizes and names of the defined arrays and we can set different values to these preprocessor definitions without having to change the source code of the program found in the `main.cpp` file.

Listing 244.
~/c++/sources/chapter_02_02_00/elif_01/main.cpp#4

```
int main() {
```

This line specifies the entry point into our **C++** program. This is effectively a definition of the C function `main`, which returns an integer `int` as the result and in our case is without `()` input parameters. At the end of the line, we use the opening brace { to indicate that the description of the body of the function begins after it. The corresponding closing brace } indicates the end of the function body description.

Listing 245.
~/c++/sources/chapter_02_02_00/elif_01/main.cpp#5

```cpp
for (int index = 0; index < ARRAY_SIZE; ++index) {
```

The first line from the beginning of the function describes a for loop with an initial integer int index zero index = 0 which is executed until the index is less than the size of the array index < ARRAY_SIZE and after each execution of the body of loop we increment the index by ++index unit. The opening curly brace { at the end of the line indicates the beginning of the body of the loop, which ends until the corresponding closing curly brace }. Initialization, validation, and index incrementing in the loop header are separated by the semicolon ; .

Listing 246.
~/c++/sources/chapter_02_02_00/elif_01/main.cpp#6

```cpp
// Set array value:
```

The first line of the body of the for loop is a **C++**

comment that specifies that the next line sets a value to an array element.

Listing 247.
~/c++/sources/chapter_02_02_00/elif_01/main.cpp#7

```
ARRAY[index] = index * index;
```

The second line of the body of the for loop sets a value to an element of the array ARRAY[index], which is the index * index square of the corresponding array index.

Listing 248.
~/c++/sources/chapter_02_02_00/elif_01/main.cpp#9

```
// Print array value:
```

The fourth line of the body of the for loop is a comment that explains that the next three lines output the value stored in an array element.

Listing 249.
~/c++/sources/chapter_02_02_00/elif_01/main.cpp#10

```
std::cout << "array[" << index << "] = " << ARRAY[index];
```

The fifth line of the body of the for loop outputs to the program console std::cout << the element with the index of the array, the equals sign, and the value of the element itself.

Listing 250.
~/c++/sources/chapter_02_02_00/elif_01/main.cpp#11

```
std::cout << "\t// <-- (" << index << " * " << index << ")";
```

The sixth line of the body of the for loop outputs to the program console std::cout << an explanation of how the value of the array element was obtained in the case of the squared array index.

Listing 251.
~/c++/sources/chapter_02_02_00/elif_01/main.cpp#12

```
std::cout << std::endl;
```

The seventh line of the body of the for loop outputs to the program console std::cout << the newline character std::endl, while at the same time outputting all the characters accumulated so far in the console buffer, if some have not yet been brought to the screen.

3.5. else_01/preprocess.hpp

Listing 252.
`~/c++/sources/chapter_02_03_00/else_01/preprocess.hpp`

```
// #define ARRAY_SIZE1 12
#define ARRAY_SIZE2 10

#if defined(ARRAY_SIZE1)
double first_array[ARRAY_SIZE1];
#define ARRAY_SIZE ARRAY_SIZE1
#define ARRAY first_array
#else
int second_array[ARRAY_SIZE2];
#define ARRAY_SIZE ARRAY_SIZE2
#define ARRAY second_array
#endif
```

Listing 253. `preprocess.hpp#1`

```
// #define ARRAY_SIZE1 12
```

We set an array size definition that we have commented out so that it is not involved in compiling the program.

Listing 254. `preprocess.hpp#2`

```
#define ARRAY_SIZE2 10
```

We set one more array size definition that will be used when compiling the program.

Listing 255. `preprocess.hpp#4`

```
#if defined(ARRAY_SIZE1)
```

Start of conditional preprocessor statement `#if`. The expression `defined(ARRAY_SIZE1)` checks if we have a preprocessor definition `ARRAY_SIZE1` defined. In this particular case, we don't because our definition is not processed by the compiler since we marked it as a comment. The preprocessor function `defined` returns `1` or `0` depending on whether the name in the parentheses is defined or not, in which case it returns `0`.

Listing 256. `preprocess.hpp#5`

```
double first_array[ARRAY_SIZE1];
```

This is the first line of the body of the conditional `#if` preprocessor statement. Here we define an array `first_array` of real numbers with double precision `double` and size `ARRAY_SIZE1`. In this particular case, this part of the code will not be compiled because the condition of the `#if` preprocessor statement is not met.

Listing 257. `preprocess.hpp#6`

```
#define ARRAY_SIZE ARRAY_SIZE1
```

This is the second line of the body of the conditional `#if` preprocessor statement. Here we set the size `ARRAY_SIZE` of the array that will be used in the program. This part of the code will not be compiled because the condition of the preprocessor `#if` statement is not met.

Listing 258. `preprocess.hpp#7`

```
#define ARRAY first_array
```

This is the third line of the body of the conditional `#if` preprocessor statement. Here we name the array that will be used in the program as `ARRAY`. This part of the code will also not be compiled because the condition of the preprocessor `#if` statement is not met.

Listing 259. `preprocess.hpp#8`

```
#else
```

This is the alternative statement `#else` whose body is checked when the condition of the statement `#if` is not met. This part of the code will be compiled because the condition of the

preprocessor statement #if is not met, i.e.
ARRAY_SIZE1 is not defined by the preprocessor
somewhere in the code before the current
check.

Listing 260. `preprocess.hpp#9`

```cpp
int second_array[ARRAY_SIZE2];
```

This is the first line of the body of the
alternative #else preprocessor statement. Here
we define an array second_array of integers int
and size ARRAY_SIZE2. In this particular case, this
part of the code will be compiled because the
condition of the #if preprocessor statement is
not met.

Listing 261. `preprocess.hpp#10`

```cpp
#define ARRAY_SIZE ARRAY_SIZE2
```

This is the second line of the body of the
alternative preprocessor #else statement. Here
we set the size ARRAY_SIZE of the array that will
be used in the program. This part of the code
will be compiled because the condition of the
#if preprocessor statement is not met.

Listing 262. `preprocess.hpp#11`

```
#define ARRAY second_array
```

This is the third line of the body of the alternative preprocessor #else statement. Here we name the array that will be used in the program as ARRAY. This part of the code will also be compiled because the condition of the preprocessor #if statement is not met.

Listing 263. `preprocess.hpp#12`

```
#endif
```

The preprocessor statement #endif specifies the end of one of the conditional preprocessor statements #if or #ifdef. In this case, it also indicates the end of the body of the alternative #else preprocessor statement.

3.6. else_01/main.cpp

Listing 264.
~/c++/sources/chapter_02_03_00/else_01/main.cpp

```cpp
#include <iostream>
#include "preprocess.hpp"

int main() {
  for (int index = 0; index < ARRAY_SIZE; ++index) {
    // Set array value:
    ARRAY[index] = index * index;

    // Print array value:
    std::cout << "array[" << index << "] = " << ARRAY[index];
    std::cout << "\t// <-- (" << index << " * " << index << ")";
    std::cout << std::endl;
  }
}
```

In practice, this program uses a loop to fill the array with the squares of its indices ARRAY[index] = index * index and output the filled values to the screen.

Let us consider the meaning of each line of it.

Listing 265.
~/c++/sources/chapter_02_03_00/else_01/main.cpp#1

```cpp
#include <iostream>
```

This line uses the #include preprocessor directive to load the stream handler definitions from the iostream file containing their descriptions. In our case, we use the std::cout, <<, and std::endl operators, with the help of which we display messages on the screen in the text console from which we run the program. The `iostream` library is part of the **Standard Template Library (STL)** of **C++**.

Listing 266.
~/c++/sources/chapter_02_03_00/else_01/main.cpp#2

```
#include "preprocess.hpp"
```

This line uses the `#include` preprocessor directive to load the definitions we've specified to use in our program from the `preprocess.hpp` file containing their descriptions. In our case, we use the preprocessor definitions `ARRAY_SIZE` and `ARRAY`. As we can see they hide the specific sizes and names of the defined arrays and we can set different values to these preprocessor definitions without having to change the source code of the program found in the `main.cpp` file.

Listing 267.
~/c++/sources/chapter_02_03_00/else_01/main.cpp#4

```
int main() {
```

This line specifies the entry point into our **C++** program. This is effectively a definition of the `C` function `main`, which returns an integer `int` as the result and in our case is without `()` input parameters. At the end of the line, we use the opening brace { to indicate that the description of the body of the function begins after it. The corresponding closing brace } indicates the end of the function body description.

```cpp
for (int index = 0; index < ARRAY_SIZE; ++index) {
```

The first line from the beginning of the function describes a for loop with an initial integer int index zero index = 0, which is executed until the index is less than the size of the array index < ARRAY_SIZE and after each execution of the body of loop we increment the index by ++index unit. The opening curly brace { at the end of the line indicates the beginning of the body of the loop, which ends until the corresponding closing curly brace }. Initialization, validation, and index incrementing in the loop header are separated by the semicolon ;.

```cpp
// Set array value:
```

The first line of the body of the for loop is a C++

comment that specifies that the next line sets a value to an array element.

Listing 270.
~/c++/sources/chapter_02_03_00/else_01/main.cpp#7

```
ARRAY[index] = index * index;
```

The second line of the body of the for loop sets a value to an element of the array ARRAY[index], which is the index * index square of the corresponding array index.

Listing 271.
~/c++/sources/chapter_02_03_00/else_01/main.cpp#9

```
// Print array value:
```

The fourth line of the body of the for loop is a comment that explains that the next three lines output the value stored in an array element.

Listing 272.
~/c++/sources/chapter_02_03_00/else_01/main.cpp#10

```
std::cout << "array[" << index << "] = " << ARRAY[index];
```

The fifth line of the body of the for loop outputs to the program console std::cout << the element with the index of the array, the equals sign, and the value of the element itself.

Listing 273.
~/c++/sources/chapter_02_03_00/else_01/main.cpp#11

```
std::cout << "\t// <-- (" << index << " * " << index << ")";
```

The sixth line of the body of the for loop outputs to the program console std::cout << an explanation of how the value of the array element was obtained in the case of the squared array index.

Listing 274.
~/c++/sources/chapter_02_03_00/else_01/main.cpp#12

```
std::cout << std::endl;
```

The seventh line of the body of the for loop outputs to the program console std::cout << the newline character std::endl, while at the same time outputting all the characters accumulated so far in the console buffer, if some have not yet been brought to the screen.

Appendix A: Installing a newer release version of the GNU Compiler Collection (GCC)

 Keep the following feature in mind before you decide to install this version!

Compiling and installing **GCC** from the source can take several hours.

1. First, we need to update the version of **Linux**:

   Listing 275. Linux Terminal

   ```
   sudo apt -y update
   ```

2. Next, we install the tools, by default for the version of the **Linux Ubuntu** operating system used, to compile **C/C++** programs.

Listing 276. Linux Terminal

```
sudo apt -y install build-essential
```

3. We also will install the following two applications - `flex` and `bison`, which are used when compiling **GCC**.

Listing 277. Linux Terminal

```
sudo apt -y install flex
sudo apt -y install bison
```

4. We enter the root folder of the current **Linux** user.

Listing 278. Linux Terminal

```
cd ~
```

5. We download the archive containing the relevant **GCC** release version and unzip it.

Listing 279. Linux Terminal

```
wget -nc \
  https://bigsearcher.com/mirrors/gcc/releases/gcc-12.2.0/gcc-12.2.0.tar.gz

tar xvzf gcc-12.2.0.tar.gz
```

 You can look at https://bigsearcher.com/mirrors/gcc/releases for a newer version.

6. We go into the just unzipped folder containing the **GCC** release.

Listing 280. Linux Terminal

```
cd gcc-12.2.0
```

7. We download the necessary dependencies to compile **GCC**.

Listing 281. Linux Terminal

```
./contrib/download_prerequisites
```

8. We export two environment variables `LIBRARY_PATH` and `LD_LIBRARY_PATH` which are required when compiling **GCC**.

Listing 282. Linux Terminal

```
export LIBRARY_PATH=/usr/lib64
export LD_LIBRARY_PATH=/usr/lib64
```

9. We create the `build` folder that we will use to build the applications from **GCC** and then enter it.

Listing 283. Linux Terminal

```
mkdir build
cd build/
```

10. We configure the system so that its creation is possible.

Listing 284. Linux Terminal

```
../configure --prefix=/usr/local/gxx-12 --disable-multilib
```

11. Starting the **GCC** build process.

Listing 285. Linux Terminal

```
time make -j $(nproc)
```

 It may take several hours depending on the power of the computer on which we run it.

12. We start the process of installing the already compiled **GCC** applications.

Listing 286. Linux Terminal

```
sudo make install
```

13. We check the current version of g++

Listing 287. Linux Terminal

```
g++ --version
```

Example 41. The command displays the current version of g++ and the result is something like this:

```
g++ (Ubuntu 11.3.0-1ubuntu1~22.04) 11.3.0
Copyright (C) 2021 Free Software Foundation, Inc.
This is free software; see the source for copying conditions.  There is
NO
warranty; not even for MERCHANTABILITY or FITNESS FOR A PARTICULAR
PURPOSE.
```

14. We insert the path to the applications from the newly built **GCC** at the beginning of the

PATH environment variable, append it to the end of the ~/.bashrc file, and finally enable the contents of this file again, enabling the new value of the PATH variable.

Listing 288. Linux Terminal

```
cd ~
echo -e "\nPATH=/usr/local/gxx-12/bin:\$PATH" >> .bashrc
source .bashrc
```

15. Again we check the current version of c++ and it should match the newly built one.

Listing 289. Linux Terminal

```
g++ --version
```

Example 42. The command displays the latest version of **GCC**, *and the result of it is something like this:*

```
g++ (GCC) 12.2.0
Copyright (C) 2022 Free Software Foundation, Inc.
This is free software; see the source for copying conditions.   There is
NO
warranty; not even for MERCHANTABILITY or FITNESS FOR A PARTICULAR
PURPOSE.
```

This completes the installation of a newer release version of **GCC**.

Appendix B: Installing the latest version of the GNU Compiler Collection (GCC)

Keep the following features in mind before you decide to install this version!

1. Compiling and installing **GCC** from the source can take several hours.
2. The latest version of **GCC** is experimental and may sometimes not compile or work completely as expected.

1. First, we need to update the version of **Linux**:

Listing 290. Linux Terminal

```
sudo apt -y update
```

2. Next, we install the tools, by default for the

version of the **Linux Ubuntu** operating system used, to compile **C/C++** programs.

Listing 291. Linux Terminal

```
sudo apt -y install build-essential
```

3. We also will install the version control system **git**, with which we will download the repository containing the latest version of **GCC**.

Listing 292. Linux Terminal

```
sudo apt -y install git
```

4. We also will install the following two applications - `flex` and `bison`, which are used when compiling **GCC**.

Listing 293. Linux Terminal

```
sudo apt -y install flex
sudo apt -y install bison
```

5. We enter the root folder of the current **Linux** user.

Listing 294. Linux Terminal

```
cd ~
```

6. We download the repository containing the latest version of **GCC**.

Listing 295. Linux Terminal

```
git clone git://gcc.gnu.org/git/gcc.git
```

7. We go into the **GCC** source code repository we just downloaded.

Listing 296. Linux Terminal

```
cd gcc/
```

8. We download the necessary dependencies to compile **GCC**.

Listing 297. Linux Terminal

```
./contrib/download_prerequisites
```

9. We export two environment variables `LIBRARY_PATH` and `LD_LIBRARY_PATH` which are required when compiling **GCC**.

Listing 298. Linux Terminal

```
export LIBRARY_PATH=/usr/lib64
export LD_LIBRARY_PATH=/usr/lib64
```

10. We create the `build` folder that we will use to build the applications from **GCC** and then enter it.

Listing 299. Linux Terminal

```
mkdir build
cd build/
```

11. We configure the system so that its creation is possible.

   Listing 300. Linux Terminal

   ```
   ../configure --prefix=/usr/local/gxx-13 --disable-multilib
   ```

12. Starting the **GCC** build process.

   Listing 301. Linux Terminal

   ```
   time make -j $(nproc)
   ```

    It may take several hours depending on the power of the computer on which we run it. The build process may fail as this is an experimental release, so you must switch to a transient tag from the git repository.

13. We start the process of installing the already compiled **GCC** applications.

   Listing 302. Linux Terminal

   ```
   sudo make install
   ```

14. We check the current version of g++.

   Listing 303. Linux Terminal

   ```
   g++ --version
   ```

Example 43. The command displays the current version of g++ *and the result is something like this:*

```
g++ (Ubuntu 11.3.0-1ubuntu1~22.04) 11.3.0
Copyright (C) 2021 Free Software Foundation, Inc.
This is free software; see the source for copying conditions.  There is
NO
warranty; not even for MERCHANTABILITY or FITNESS FOR A PARTICULAR
PURPOSE.
```

15. We insert the path to the applications from the newly built **GCC** at the beginning of the PATH environment variable, append it to the end of the ~/.bashrc file, and finally enable the contents of this file again, enabling the new value of the PATH variable.

Listing 304. Linux Terminal

```
cd ~
echo -e "\nPATH=/usr/local/gxx-13/bin:\$PATH" >> .bashrc
source .bashrc
```

16. Again we will check the current version of the C++ compiler and it should match the newly built one.

Listing 305. Linux Terminal

```
g++ --version
```

Example 44. The command displays the latest version of **GCC**, *and the result of it is something like this:*

```
g++ (GCC) 14.0.1 20240130 (experimental)
```

This completes the installation of the latest experimental version of **GCC**.

About the Author

Eng. Zlatin Georgiev

https://www.linkedin.com/in/zlatin-georgiev/

Dear reader,
You can write about this book to Zlatin Georgiev

by e-mail:
zlatin.v.g@gmail.com

with the subject:
Fast and Easy C++ Lessons: In This Edition
Preprocessing On Microsoft Visual Studio Code
in Linux Ubuntu

Of course, the author will not be able to respond to all e-mails, but he will consider your recommendations regarding the content of this book if possible.

Other books from the series til now

- Fast and Easy C++ Lessons: In This Edition Bitwise Operators On Microsoft Visual Studio Code in Linux Ubuntu
- Fast and Easy C++ Lessons: In This Edition Bitwise Operators On Microsoft Visual Studio Code in Windows
- Fast and Easy C++ Lessons: In This Edition Character Sets On Microsoft Visual Studio Code in Linux Ubuntu
- Fast and Easy C++ Lessons: In This Edition Character Sets On Microsoft Visual Studio Code in Windows
- Fast and Easy C++ Lessons: In This Edition Preprocessing On Microsoft Visual Studio Code in Linux Ubuntu
- Fast and Easy C++ Lessons: In This Edition Preprocessing On Microsoft Visual Studio Code in Windows

All books have the following formats:

1. Color interior:
   - Kindle

- Paperback
- Hardcover

2. Black and white interior:
   - Paperback
   - Hardcover

www.ingramcontent.com/pod-product-compliance
Lightning Source LLC
Chambersburg PA
CBHW050806290526
45792CB00001B/3